Pieces Left for the Morning

Alexandria

Pieces Left for the Morning

Olympia Publishers
London

www.olympiapublishers.com
OLYMPIA PAPERBACK EDITION

Copyright © Alexandria 2024

The right of Alexandria to be identified as author of
this work has been asserted in accordance with sections 77 and 78 of
the Copyright, Designs and Patents Act 1988.

All Rights Reserved

No reproduction, copy or transmission of this publication
may be made without written permission.
No paragraph of this publication may be reproduced,
copied or transmitted save with the written permission of the publisher,
or in accordance with the provisions
of the Copyright Act 1956 (as amended).

Any person who commits any unauthorized act in relation to
this publication may be liable to criminal
prosecution and civil claims for damage.

A CIP catalogue record for this title is
available from the British Library.

ISBN: 978-1-80439-702-2

This is a work of fiction.
Names, characters, places and incidents originate from the writer's
imagination. Any resemblance to actual persons, living or dead, is
purely coincidental.

First Published in 2024

Olympia Publishers
Tallis House
2 Tallis Street
London
EC4Y 0AB

Printed in Great Britain

Dedication

To all the ones who hurt me.
To the one who saved me.
To the friend who always listened.
To the mistakes I've made.
To self-love.

I have poured my heart into these words.
Emotions that have been kept in for so long now have the chance to speak to others.
Oh, what a day to be alive.

To Whom It No Longer Concerns

Beautiful smiles cover wicked truths.
Curses in the form of loving words.
A witch in the form of a savior.

Love should not be blamed for the actions of a person.
This emotion cannot make someone hurt you.

Young minds do not see who is right or wrong,
they only see the fight.

The young girl was loved,
she just knew someone was missing.

Minds are shaped from an early age.
Please tell the little ones they are loved.

With each passing birthday the girl grew.
She got taller and her mind got sharper.
She saw people for who they were,
not what they told her they were.

The older man replaced the father she never knew.
His name was never spoken.

The older woman loved the small girl as her own.
Covering for the one who gave the child life.
The older woman showed love, where the other did not show at all.

Manipulating lies cover fragile truths.
Judgment in the woman's eyes could not be hidden.
The woman could not love her creation, this the young girl knew.

The small girl believed the woman would return.
The girl blamed the postage for no birthday cards and the
phone company for no
calls.
Deep down the small girl knew the woman was to blame,
but the girl loved her so.
She
loved the woman she did not know.

I'm sorry.
Sorry.
I am sorry.
The power behind one word can change the course of a life.

Sometimes the girl longs to hear the woman's voice,
to see the woman's face.
A longing for a feeling rather than the actual person.

A letter you will never read:
Dearest Villain, I win.

She prayed for answers, hoping for closure.
The woman who haunts her, who plagues her,
who created her.
How could this woman not love her?

With staggered breaths and hopeless feelings,
she held a torch to the bridge and watched it burn.

Watching from afar the love is thick.
A love the girl does not know though the words she has been told.
She can never understand why she was met with rejection or why she was left.
The young girl longed to feel like the others, but the feeling never showed.

Heartbreak doesn't always come from a lover.

My guilt no longer
I gave you my trust and you broke it.
I gave you my love and you denied it.
This is on you.

A Letter Collecting Dust

There are so many things that I want to say to you, so many things I want to know.
Forgiveness hasn't been an easy choice for me, I still struggle with it.
I still feel the anger in my soul and heartache in my bones.
Somedays I wish I had you to give me advice and to talk to.
Those are the days that I miss you the most.
Other days I avoid mirrors, so I don't have to see your face and avoid laughing so I don't have to hear your voice.
It's a complex feeling, to love someone and despise them all at the same time.
I wish you knew what you have done to me, how broken I've been because of you.
I've spent years stripping away my layers to find what is wrong with me.
To find the thing that made me so unlovable.
How does the one who gave you life become your first heartbreak?
If you would have stayed away, I would have been better off.
You convinced me to love you and to trust you, then you betrayed me.

I am in no way perfect, nor have I ever been, but no one deserves to feel like this.
No one deserves this kind of pain.
You made me scared of trust, made me shy of love. What you considered a game, I considered my life.
I was young and looking for your guidance and acceptance and
all I found was confusion and grief.
You made me the shell of the person I wanted to be.
You took my light, but I finally got it back. I've found pieces of me along this journey that I never knew existed.
I've made myself proud and deep down I wish you knew me now.
I wish you could see the person I have become.
I'm sorry for whoever hurt you,
for whoever made you feel like love wasn't an option and broke you in this way.
It's time I let go though,
of this hurt and anger I feel inside.
This is the last time I will write about you.
I wish you all the love I deserved.
Love Always,
The girl with your eyes

The Heart Featured on the Back of the Milk Carton

His touch felt as warm as summer,
but his heart remained as cold as an icy winter.

A plague of locusts could not do as much damage as you have done to my heart.
No life support can bring back the pieces of me your betrayal murdered.
Like an artifact from a mummy's tomb you cursed me, haunting me to the brink of madness.

The greatest sound I have ever heard was the door closing behind you as you left.

Kiss me a thousand times,
but it won't take away what you have done.
You have hidden hatred behind the illusion of love.
One, two, three, hits each more painful than the last.
This is what you have made us.
What was innocent and new is now tainted and worn.
You have become the darkness you ran so long from.

Mask your insecurities with lies.
Tell the world you are the hero, the one who saves the day.
Stroke your ego and build your pride.
Every villain goes through the pretend hero phase.

I loved you, even when my heart was breaking because of you

You are the unspoken name that lines the pages of my journal.

She loved him, but was too afraid to let him in.
He knocked and knocked but she kept the curtains drawn.

Tales from an Addict

When most people think of an addiction
they think of drugs, but for some addiction is a person.
The way they move or tell sweet lies.
The high of possibilities and longing.
When toxic words fall from a desired mouth rehabilitation is nowhere in sight.

The Abuser

With every strike, he promised love.

He was poison disguised as the cure.

NO.
No other explanation is needed when this word is spoken.

Now that she has left you want her back.
That's not how this works,
you don't mistreat someone then claim to love them.

Purple the color of lust.

We began as friends and ended as strangers.

They said goodbye a hundred times only for their paths to cross once more.

Tales of an Abuser

Never again he swore, chaos brewing in him.
Like watching an angel and demon fight over their host,
she prayed the angel would win.

No Regrets

Small smiles in passing and long stares from afar.
The two were playing with fire ready to be burned.

& one day you were gone.

She searched every letter looking for evidence of love in the words he wrote.

Nothing hurts worse than the exact moment a heart breaks.

Just in Time

Muffled screams echo through a hot palm.
Fear covering all thoughts.
For a moment her body is not her own, the word no has zero meaning.
Gripping reality and a monster's whisper fill her head with what is to come.
An opening door and a stranger save her from the vile fate that awaited her.
She was lucky, the stranger was just in time.

Oh, to be so many things to one person.
A stranger
A friend
Their calm
Their lover
Their passion
Their worry
Their heartbreak
A stranger.

He begged her to stay like she begged him to stop with every assault.

They agreed never again in between tangled sheets, knowing their clothes would share a spot together on the floor once more.

He loved her, just not in the way that was good for her.

He was an addiction.
The highest grade of drugs.
The top shelf of liquor,
but she continued to love him anyway.
That's how love works,
we take the bait knowing the outcome.

Clothes on the floor & regret in the air.

In the corner of a house her worst fear almost came true.
When a person does not take no for an answer and reveals truest evil.
If not for the angel disguised as a stranger this would be a different tale.

He hits her, but swears he loves her.
Abuse masked by the illusion of love.

She gave him something she could never get back and he took it with the slyest grin.

Save me she whispered, I can't he replied.

Sometimes the one who saves you also breaks you.

"At least I got to see you one more time."
...how that broke her heart.

He loved her but he wasn't in love with her.
He asked her to stay anyway, fearful of being alone.
She knew this game; she had played it for far too long.

The wild-eyed boy set a fire inside the girl.
Giving promises of love and happiness.
Though the promises he did not keep, he gave her
something more valuable.
He gave her the thirst for life.
Because of the wild-eyed boy, she would no longer settle.

He visits her in her dreams,
showing her a life that was never meant to be.
A tease in the dream, a heartbreak in reality.

She loved him and he loved her, but timing was never on their side.

He was beautiful, but his beauty was wicked.
It tricked the girl,
making her believe they could be more.
Making her believe that love was all that mattered.

She searched back through her memories looking for his face.
Proof a broken heart can come in many forms.

Only her sheets know their secrets.

You wait for me behind my eyelids each night.
Dreams of far-off memories in the night.

Sometimes we break our own hearts.
We think of people after they have left us.
We listen to songs that make us think of memories.
We relive the hurt to feel time close to us again.
Sometimes we are our own source of pain.

He haunts her in her dreams.
Taunting her with scenarios that never came to pass.
He speaks words that were never said.
He haunts her with dreams of what could have been.

It was in that parking lot that she knew he was the one.
She did not know if he was the one to love her,
save her or break her heart.
She just knew this was the moment that everything changed.

Words are such powerful things.
They have the power to heal a soul or break a heart.

Don't let loneliness drive you into the arms of someone you don't love.

Sometimes our heart knows it's over before we are willing to accept it.

Moving on means seeing them on the street and not feeling
a change in your
body as they pass you by.
Moving on is one of the greatest feats of the heart.

An odd thing is that the body part that beats for us is the one that breaks the easiest.

Tales from a Worn Soul

The girl was loved.
The girl was broken.
The girl was alone.
The girl mourned.
The girl turned into a woman.
The woman had a heart of stone.

Hot water pours from the shower giving way to hot skin.
Turning up the heat she longs to feel.
Her heart has turned cold.
Numbness has made a home in her body.
Her eyes cannot hide the truth any longer.
The hot water continues to fall, washing away another day and making way for another sleepless night.

Stained cheeks gave away her sadness like a dirty secret.
Her shaking hands told the story of her fears.
The girl was broken you see, she just didn't want the world to know.

She built her walls so high no one could climb them.
She guarded herself so no one could enter.
The girl who had loved for so long had grown distant.
The girl had no intention of returning.

Anxiety

A thousand pounds on her chest and a veil over her eyes.
The spell will pass but leave its mark.
She hides the truth because she fears judgment.
Thousands of people feel the same, but this she will never know.

If it were to ever be released her rage would tear the world apart.

Years of buried emotions have turned the beautiful girl dark.

The sound of rain has silenced her mind.
The clouds have taken on a new shade of gray.
The depression has subsided but is never far away.

It happened slowly, then suddenly.
Losing yourself sneaks up on you.
One day you look in the mirror and are startled by the stranger you see.

Sadness lurks behind her smile.
It has made a home in her soul.

I am too young to feel so many years bearing down on my soul.

Crying is not the worst.
It's the silence that comes after.

Rage is not made overnight; it is grown overtime.
From the parent who left,
to the boy who hits when angered.
When there is no love, rage plants roots.
It spreads like a weed, until there is nothing left,
until everything is covered.

The night leaves her in pieces.
Leaving the morning to put her back together.

The darkness calls to her, how long before she will answer.

Every night she faces the same choice.
Does she lay awake and stare into the darkness or fall asleep and let it consume her.

Sometimes it all feels too much.
The world moves at a fast pace.
The days move by with no accomplishments to mention.
Sometimes it feels as though I was meant for a slower time,
a time when the day waited on a person to find themselves.

Anger has no voice of reason.

Anxiety's Voice

Walking on a tightrope waiting to fall.
How long will I spiral?

My mind was unsure of my writings, they reeked of my heart.

Depression

Curtains drawn to hide the sunny day.
Emojis used to cover the sadness in her words.
A hot shower to mask the falling tears.
In the brightest room shadows still lurk,
darkness holds her hand.
No one will ever know how broken she feels, her smiling
face hides her secret well.

The past sentences her to eternal torment.
Whispers of rejection float around her head.
Battle scars mark memories like a road map.
This darkness harbors in her bones, fighting any light that dare enter.

The night sings sweet songs to cover the loneliness that waits.

She looks in the mirror, searching for a face she will recognize.

We all play our parts.
The sun plays tag with the clouds, the moon flirts with the stars.
Our universe is odd in that way.
We all love and lose;
We play games like cat and mouse and expect to win.

Sometimes I worry my pillowcase may drown in all the tears it has caught.

Everyone has darkness, just different demons.

Liquor burns her lips as she takes another sip.
Liquid fire to drown out the darkness.
Another night of foggy memories and blurry walls.
Sometimes feeling something is better than feeling nothing at all.

Her mind runs its fastest races when the night has grown silent.

Snap Out of It

Reality is hard to come back to when the fantasy is so good.
A place for safety to feel normal.
A place for desires to be met.
Is this a place to stay forever?

Somewhere between the hello and goodbye
I found myself and lost myself all at the same time.

The seasons change.
The leaves change colors, the flowers bloom.
Our universe changes constantly,
but some people choose to remain the same.

It all happens in the dark of night.
When the silence takes over and
when thoughts come out to play.
The darkness shows us our dreams, fears,
and makes us face who we really are.

That's the thing about expectations, not many people can live up to them.

The hardest part about giving up is never knowing what would have happened if you would have tried for one more day.

She hid her fear like a stolen item.
Within her she buried it deep,
knowing there it would never see the light of day.

Sleepless nights have become a part of my routine.
A slow and steady descent into spirals of my mind.
Darkness lurks in the crevasses and
self-doubt forms an alliance with insecurities.
In the midst of the battle being fought in my head
I can't help but wonder what I did to deserve this carnage.

I can phantom that the ocean is so deep that unknown creatures lurk in its darkness.
I can comprehend that space is vast and mysterious.
All of these things I can process, but I still can't believe that I am loved.

Somewhere between sixteen and nineteen
I turned forty-five.
I have grown past my years,
living life in ways I wouldn't wish on others.
Heart breaks and rejection cling to my lost years
like a prized treasure.
Despair stole my minutes and abuse held my hours captive.
I have seen the worst in people and in myself,
hoping for light in the maze of endless darkness.

She knew the mistakes she had made.
She remembered what she was told and what she was called.
With that, she made the decision that she was undeserving of love, so she fled.
She fled to the most remote parts of herself, shutting others out so they did not feel her cold.

Her right wrist carries a perfectly round scar. Faded now, only noticeable when searched for, but the memory still burns.

She can be in a room full of people
&
still feel the breath of loneliness.

Self-Love, A Beautiful Thing

They ask me how I overcame it.
How I found a new me in the debris of my older pieces.
The answer is simple,
I looked for the person I wanted my mother to be.

She felt her anger.
Like a volcano waiting to erupt.
She felt the heat on her cheeks and the rumble in her palms.
Not knowing how much longer she could contain it she did
the only thing she knew to do.
Forgive.

The world is cruel, but she is tough.

She pulled herself from the ground and decided she would take no more.
The princess laid down her crown for a sword.

She didn't need to be saved.
She needed a realization.

No woman should have to feel the hate of another woman.
Let us build each other up, not tumble over jealousy.

A word to the wise: You must forgive.
It's the only way to set yourself free.

Love yourself so fiercely that even the stars are jealous.

Hero Talk

She tucks her thoughts away and seals her lips.
She will be the one everyone wants her to be.
She will slay everyone else's dragons and then her own.

This is the part of the story where she saves herself.

You Can Shine

The stars shine so brightly, giving away the moon's secrets.
Dancing shadows in and out of alleyways.
There maybe nights where the moon isn't always whole,
but it still manages to shine.

Stop looking for someone to love you.
No other person can save you when you're drowning.
My darling, you are your own savior.

Don't let your rage be their fuel.

She was magic once she realized her worth.

She has waited years to hear the words she just told herself.
You are loved.

Like a balloon floating through the sky.
She was free.

Forgive yourself.
Perfection is only a word.

In between the pencil smudges and the tear stains was a
journal full of emotions.
Each page told a secret or revealed a fear.
Heartache fell off the pages and hope lingered on each word.
She rebuilt herself within the walls of this journal.

The pain you feel right now, don't bury it.
This pain will not end you.
This pain will not define you.
You are so much more than this one emotion.

Choices

She loved him, but she loved herself more.

She gave her all to the world, hoping it would do the same in return.

She looked to the stars for guidance.
Surely something so beautiful has the answers.

She buried herself in the words she wrote.
Confessions covered the pages and memories labeled by page numbers.
This book knew more about her than any other person ever has.

Sometimes pain is the first step towards healing.

Let the anger end with you.
Do not paint your emotions upon others.
Do not sentence the innocent to your demons.
Let this rage not affect the ones who help carry your burden.

People who write poetry have seen the world in many colors.
To write is to feel and leave a piece of yourself on the page.

Do not let someone lessen your emotions.
You have the right to what you want and need to feel.

She picked up the shattered pieces of herself that were scattered on the floor like confetti.
With those pieces she built herself into the amazing woman she knew she could be.

She rebuilt herself.
She used the silence to conquer her demons.
She used car rides to sort her thoughts.
She used bookstores to calm her.
She rebuilt herself into the person she always intended to be.

Like a lilac ready to bloom,
she showed the world her beauty.

Be brave.
Be courageous.
Be whatever you need to be to see the worth that you are.

They spent so much time explaining how the world works
that they forgot to tell us
how beautiful we are.

When you look in the mirror, know that the person looking back at you is a warrior.
A goddess with the power to change the world.

Take a shower and wash away the day's discomforts. Tomorrow is new and waiting for you.

Music speaks when we have grown silent.
Words that can express how we feel in the moment of
uncertainty,
in the moment of clarity.
Music speaks if we listen.

I have loved, lost, and found something new all within the words of a book.
I have traveled to new lands and seen magic in the most remote places of the world.
Within a book I found both comfort and adventure.

Love Becoming

He saved her.
Not from anyone but herself.

To love someone is beautiful, but to be in love with someone is pure magic.

She kissed away his fears and put to bed his doubts.
Maybe she couldn't save herself, but she would try her best
to save him.

Unravel Me

Undo all of the pieces that hold my sanity together and let me go crazy in your love.
Unravel the parts that shy away from happiness, give them a home in your heart.
Unravel the stitched-up pieces that take away the beauty and let me see all
that you have to offer.
Unravel me so that I am yours.

Isn't it beautiful?
The way heartbreak reveals raw pain.
The way love stirs the soul's deepest desires.
All of this and some still don't believe in magic.

Play any song and I will find you in it.

He was green forest in mountainous terrain.
So simple, but so rich with life.
I could watch him for hours doing nothing extraordinary,
just existing.

My heart loved you before I even knew your name.

I will love you like I should have loved myself for all of these years.

How lucky we are to find a person to share this short life with.
To share the moments that hurt us and then the moments that make us glad to be alive.
How lucky we are to find a person that fits in our soul so perfectly.

Blessed with a loving soul he showed her how to love with an open heart.

She loses herself in the thought of him.

He's the light at the end of the tunnel.
A beacon for all that is good.
She's in awe as she watches him conquer the dark.

It was in the way that the sun followed him during the day
and the moon gazed
upon him during the night.
The world was his and he was hers.

Saving Grace

The man that sleeps beside her each night.

He is her calm, even in the roughest of seas

To love another is to give away a piece of your soul with no intention of reclaiming it.

They were made of magic.
Their love was the spell and his words the wand.

Take my hand, said the man and together they built a life of love.

His touch brings her back to life, reminding her of how it feels to feel love.
His laughter is contagious, his smile is infectious.
Could this man be the one,
could this man be the one made perfectly for her.

Inside Jokes

Her saving grace. The man she loved.
He was a dick.

She was alone, but okay with that.
She had peace with herself.
Then she met a man with hopeful eyes and an ambitious mind.
Together they would discover the meaning of true love.

She believed love was an emotion she dared not feel again, until she met him.

She sees pieces of him all around.
The way rain slides down a window.
How the sun reflects on water.
She sees pieces of him in everything beautiful.

Love is the source of pure madness

The man did not care that she had been broken in the past.
He did not care that she had once grown cold.
He loved her.
He loved her despite it all.

She would give up an eternal life just to spend one normal one with him.

Love is a necessity, whether you're giving or receiving.

He's not just a lover, he's a feeling.
The butterflies in her stomach, the calmness in her bones.
She loved him before she realized.
Like a worn book full of life, he is her comfort.
Home in the form of a person.

He carved his name into her soul.
Making sure a piece of her was always his.

He's spread across every sunset.
The beautiful ones with vibrant colors and the dark ones leading to a darker night.
He is everywhere there is to look.

She longs to be like him.
A warm cup of coffee on a cold morning.
He inhabits perfection.

The world is his canvas, I'm just his adoring fan.

Reach into my soul and you will find It's riddled with you.

I will love you today,
in this universe and the next.
This love has no bounds and no sense of time.
It's a consuming love,
a love that will never end.